Encouraging Angels

Lawrence Balleine

Encouraging Angels
ISBN: Softcover 978-1-955581-02-8
Copyright © 2021 by Lawrence Balleine

All rights reserved. No part of this book may be reproduced or transmitted in any form or by any means, electronic or mechanical, including photocopying, recording, or by any information storage and retrieval system, without permission in writing from the publisher.

www.parsonsporch.com

Encouraging Angels

Introduction

Encouraging Angels is the fourth novella in a series that documents the sabbatical journey of Michael Lattimore, a middle school social science teacher who travels to the dairy farm regions of his home state – Wisconsin. He wants to see how the changes of the past three decades have affected the average family farmer. Whereas *Entertaining Angels* is a story of change, loss and healing; *An Angel Among Us* addresses change, brokenness and reconciliation; and *Angels in Disguise* deals with change, loss and new beginnings; *Encouraging Angels* explores change, fear and encouragement.

Thursday Mid-morning

"What a difference a day makes!" It was this common assertion that pulled Michael's attention away from his nagging question as to whether the village of Colby received its name from a style of cheese it makes, or if Colby style cheese received its name from the town in which it was first produced.

"Yes indeed, the difference from yesterday to today is significant," Michael announced to himself, "and thankfully, it is a very good difference. Yesterday, Sid was a desperate man, even considering suicide as all his milk cows were being auctioned and he felt like he was losing the only life he had ever known. Today his whole attitude is completely turned around. And he's not only called the suicide hot line, he and Janice have also committed to take part in a support group for farmers undergoing similar crises." Michael paused a moment and then smiled: "I think Sid and Janice are going to be OK."

Michael had just finished sharing a tasty breakfast and good visit at the home of Sid and Janice. It was their way of showing appreciation to Michael who – on a whim -- had stopped at the auction the previous day. And there, Michael had helped Sid when he appeared to be "at his lowest," lifting Sid from the depths of his despair and allowing Sid to discover a new and positive outlook.

Michael still had a decision to make. Would he continue north and west from Colby and head toward the dairying regions of northwestern Wisconsin, or would he turn east and travel toward Wausau? He thought if he had a coin he would flip it. If heads was up, he'd initially proceed west to Eau Claire; but if the coin showed tails, he'd go eastward. But then he thought: Having just received the good news yesterday about Ali's pregnancy, the sooner I get home, the better. It's not every day you're told the exciting news that your first grandchild is on the way. Going east would knock off at least a couple of days of my trip. He was fine with that. So, he announced to himself: "Wausau, here I come."

But first, before he left the Colby area, he wanted to discover an answer to his question regarding the town of Colby and its cheese. Michael recalled seeing what he thought may have been a Co-op complex on the south side of Colby as he drove from Abbotsford – where he had spent the night – to Sid and Janice's place. He knew he could probably get an answer to his question regarding Colby and its cheese from someone at the Co-op. So, he decided he would stop there before proceeding east.

In addition to getting an answer to his "cheesy" question, he determined his goal for the day: Get at least as far as Wausau. It was less than forty miles away. But again, as in his past eight days of travel, he would take back roads and avoid major highways as much as possible. And, as he had been doing for over a week, he assumed he would be making several stops along the way as he continued his quest to determine how the cultural changes of the past thirty years or so were affecting the family dairy farm.

A few minutes later he arrived at the complex he had noticed about an hour and a half earlier. Yes, it was a Co-op, and it was located at the intersection of Highway 13 and County Highway N. That was fortuitous, for he planned to make his way toward Wausau on the less traveled two-lane County N rather than the four lane State Highway 29.

Upon entering the store, Michael walked over to the auto parts counter where he approached a fella in dark blue bib overalls. Wearing a tag identifying him as Rich and an employee of the Co-op, he called out to Michael: "Any way I can help you?"

Michael replied: "This may sound like a foolish question, but I've been wondering: Is Colby cheese named after the town of Colby, or did the village get its name from the cheese?"

Rich responded: "Obviously, you aren't from around these parts, or you'd know."

"You're right. I'm from Green Bay. By the way, I'm Michael Lattimore."

Pointing to his name tag, the auto parts salesclerk said: "As you can see, I'm Rich. And I've lived in these parts all my fifty-two years. So let me give you a little local history if that's OK with you."

"I'd be pleased if you did."

"Colby cheese was developed just down the road to the west at the old Steinwand Cheese Factory. Ambrose Steinwand had built the factory, and it was in 1885 that his son Joseph came up with the cheese that bears the name of the township in which his father's factory had been built – Colby."

"So, the cheese got its name from the township and not the other way around."

"That's correct."

Thank you," said Michael, "My curiosity is finally satisfied."

"You say you're from Green Bay. Well, I should probably tell you that Ambrose Steinwand and his family came to Colby after living in Manitowoc County."

"Really? I was born in Manitowoc County. I didn't arrive in Green Bay until a few years ago.

"Is the factory still in operation?" asked Michael.

"No. Shut down years ago."

"What about the building? Is the building still standing?" Michael inquired further.

"No. It was demolished several years ago," reported Rich.

"That's a shame. Could have made an interesting tourist stop."

"It would have been nice if someone had come up with that idea before it was torn down."

Rich continued: "Don't you have some pretty good cheese over in Green Bay?"

"We do."

"If you don't mind me asking, what are you doing over this way, Michael?"

"I've been visiting the various dairying regions in the state and asking folks – primarily dairy farmers – about how they are being affected by all the changes that they are continually facing."

"Well since we're talking about cheese, that whole industry has certainly undergone changes. Used to be you'd venture out on almost any country road and you'd find a cheese factory about every six miles," stated Rich.

"I know there was a lot more when I was a kid. But why every six miles?" asked Michael.

"That's because a half dozen miles was about how far farmers could transport their milk – usually by horse and wagon – before it would start to spoil. But with refrigeration came bulk tanks in the milk house -- usually a section added onto the barn – and refrigerated tanker trucks carrying the milk to the factories. That pretty much eliminated spoilage and allowed the raw milk to be carried farther. And so, while some cheese factories expanded, a lot of them closed. I recently read that Wisconsin had more than

2800 cheese factories in the 1920's. Now I suppose there's only about a hundred; maybe a hundred and fifty at most."

"In my travels, I've noticed a lot of former factories have been converted into residences or storage buildings. After a while, you can pretty much tell whether a building had been used as a cheese factory. In the south central and southwestern parts of the state I saw that many of the factories were built into the side of a hill. I was told this would allow the operator to bore out a good size hole in the hill, and there they would store their cheese while it aged."

Rich added: "You mentioned that some of the cheese factories have been turned into homes. You are probably aware that with many cheese factories, the cheesemaker's living quarters were found in the upper level of the building -- above the actual factory. This was especially helpful during the colder months when the heat from the factory would rise and warm the living quarters."

"That sounds pretty energy efficient to me," replied Michael.

"I don't doubt that it was."

Then Michael reflected: "As a kid, even though we had plenty of factories close by, my grandpa would often take me to a cheese factory in Kewaunee County. Unfortunately, they ceased operations some time back. I drove past the empty cinder block building about a year ago. I remember how the place smelled when they were making cheese. Do not know how folks could live in some quarters above a factory and smell that all day and night. Lately, the factories I have been in don't seem to smell as much. Either that is the case, or maybe my sniffer isn't as sensitive as it was when I was a kid.

"There's something else I've been noticing: Although there are less factories, the variety of cheeses being produced has substantially increased. When I was a kid and teen it seemed that most of the factories where I grew up in Manitowoc County, and many of those in neighboring counties, were known for their cheddar. And I know that the factories in the south-central part of the state – like in Green County – in years past almost always produced Swiss, and Limburger. Now, you never know what kind of cheese a factory is making. I know of one factory from my home area that previously only made cheddar: now they specialize in mozzarella. I have heard it's because of the frozen pizza business. Last week I stopped by one factory in Green County that at one time made only Swiss; now – Bruce, a licensed master cheesemaker and his son, Ben, also a licensed cheesemaker -- make butterkase, Havarti, and muenster in addition to Swiss. And a lot of factories do specialty cheeses – they're called artisan cheeses – and the varieties range from Havarti dill to marbled blue jack."

"So you've been traveling around the state and sampling all the cheese?" asked Rich.

"Yes; I've been traveling the state, taking the lesser traveled roads whenever possible; and yes, I've tried a lot of cheese."

"If you've been traveling the back roads, you probably noticed something else."

"What's that?" asked Michael.

"The roads. Most of them are paved," Rich informed Michael.

"Come to think of it, you're absolutely right. Are you getting at something?"

"I've heard that the reason most country roads are paved in Wisconsin is because of the dairy farms. Good roads are needed so that the milk trucks can get the raw milk to the cheese factories; or wherever else it might go."

"That's interesting; and it makes good sense. I've actually been on very few gravel roads; even the roads with only a few remaining farms have usually been asphalt."

Michael paused a moment and then continued: "Thank you for all your good information. I best be going so you can get back to what you were doing before I interrupted you."

"Well, enjoy the remainder of your travels," said Rich.

"I will; and thank you again for spending some time with me."

After Michael exited the Co-op he returned to his red Ford pickup truck. He was satisfied to have received the answer to the question that had been plaguing him: So Colby cheese gets its name from the town of Colby. Pulling a Hershey chocolate bar he had stored in his glove box, he stared at it and remarked: "So it's not like Hershey, Pennsylvania. That town got it's name from it's famous chocolate that Milton Hershey began producing in 1894."

In a moment Michael was back on the road again. As had been his practice for the past eight days and as he indicated to Rich moments earlier, he would avoid the superhighways as much as possible and proceed along the lesser traveled roads. And so, leaving Colby, he joined County Highway N and started toward Wausau.

Now on the ninth day of his sabbatical journey, Michael had assumed his road trip to Wisconsin's dairying regions would take about two weeks. But with his decision to forego the farming area around Eau Claire and locations further north, Michael was now a couple of days ahead of his very loose schedule.

Thursday Late Morning

About five or six miles down the road Michael rounded a bend and noticed a well-kept country church. A cemetery was on its left, and a house that he assumed was the parsonage or rectory stood to the right of the church building. He decided to stop. Michael doubted that the church was unlocked, but he thought: At least I can walk around the cemetery.

Wisconsin is well-known for its pockets of various ethnic groups, so Michael knew that if he looked at the names on several headstones, he would be able to determine the ethnic background of the folks living in the area. None-the-less, he would first check to see if the front door to the church was open.

As Michael parked in the small paved lot in front of the church building, he noticed a sign near the entrance to the church. It read: "St. Stanislaus Catholic Church. Saturday mass at 5 P.M. Sunday mass at 8 A.M. Fr. Theodore Janakowski, pastor." Then he noticed the church's cornerstone. It indicated that the attractive, well-kept red brick structure had been built in 1922.

Upon walking up the three front steps, Michael was surprised that when he tried to open the church's front door, he was successful. Once inside, his eyes were drawn to the beautiful stained glass windows – six on the left and six on the right. The morning sun poured through the windows on the east wall, producing a myriad of colors – reds, greens, blues, yellows, and violets – on the pews in front of him. Each window portrayed one of the original apostles. Then he noted the stations of the cross along the side walls of the sanctuary. He paused, and his eyes were drawn to the large crucifix hanging central above the altar. Then he took note of the altar itself and the elaborately carved woodwork surrounding it. He wondered if they were creations of the Svoboda Church Furniture Company of Kewaunee. Michael remembered driving past Svoboda's several times during his youth on his way to Door County. Svoboda's had operated for nearly a hundred years during which time its skilled workers had crafted the indoor wooden furnishings – including statuary, altars, facades, and pews – that adorn many churches throughout the upper Midwest.

After stepping outdoors, Michael gazed at the rectory. He sensed that it was no longer occupied by a resident priest. That is a change in rural American Catholicism, Michael thought. Many of the smaller parishes have merged to form larger parishes, and those that did not merge often share a priest with one or more nearby parishes. He assumed this was the case with Saint Stanislaus.

Then Michael walked down the steps and ambled over to the cemetery: "Malinowski, Dolski, Lewandowski" -- these were just a few of the names he noted on the tombstones. Obviously, I've come to an area that was populated by Polish settlers, thought Michael. Being a middle school social studies teacher who taught a class on Wisconsin History and Culture, he knew several folks of Polish descent settled in central Wisconsin after emigrating to the United States in the later part of the 19th century.

After walking for about ten minutes in the cemetery, Michael turned to leave. It is then that he realized that he was not the only person in the cemetery. He had not noticed when an elderly woman and a fella about Michael's age arrived. They were placing flowers on two side by side graves. Michael did not want to disturb them, so he lingered among the older gravestones located near the church building. He soon noted that the two were kneeling. Observing their hand movements, Michael assumed that they were "praying the rosary." He then saw each of them make "the sign of the cross." Then the man helped the aging woman to her feet.

Encouraging Angels

When the couple looked up, they noticed Michael and started walking toward him. As they approached, the fella called out; "Hello," he said to Michael, "You look a little lost. Did you find the grave you're looking for?"

"Well, I really wasn't looking for anyone. I was driving by and I noticed the beautiful church and the cemetery so I thought I'd get out and stretch my legs," Michael replied.

"You found a peaceful place to do it," the woman said.

"Do you come here often?" asked Michael.

"Once a month. Mom and I have been coming for the last ten years or so; before that she and dad came -- ever since my brother John was killed in Vietnam," said the fella. "We always bring flowers for Memorial Day, Independence Day and Veteran's Day. That is what we're doing today. We're bringing flowers for Independence Day weekend."

Looking at the woman, Michael interjected: "I assume this is your son," and then turning toward the man accompanying her, he asked: "Your brother was a veteran?"

"Can you call someone a veteran if they never make it back home? Killed only two weeks before his tour was up," said the fella.

"I would certainly consider your brother a veteran," offered Michael.

"It's been almost fifty years and I can still see him as he left home for the last time. He was wearing that happy-go-lucky smile of his and said: 'See you later.' That is the last time we saw him alive," said the woman.

"It must have been hard," replied Michael.

"Awful. Boyd, my late husband, and I cried for weeks. But eventually, we came to terms with it all.

The neighbors and our friends here at church were all so helpful."

The fella, putting his arm around his mom, added: "And I think it helped when mom and dad traveled to Washington – not the state, but D.C. -- and visited the Vietnam Memorial wall. They said that they wept when they finally located John's name among the over fifty-eight thousand, but it also helped them to see his name with all his comrades. They said that until they visited the Memorial Wall, they had hoped one day John would come home and walk through the door. But seeing his name on the memorial helped them to face the reality of his death. Notice I did not say that seeing his name on the wall gave them closure. First, I think the term 'closure' is overused; and second, if closure means that you complete your grieving, I just don't think that happens. You can never completely get over it – especially if it is a death like John's.

"By the way, I'm Boyd Kolski. Folks around here call me Junior. This is my mom, Helen."

"'Good to meet you. I'm Michael Lattimore."

"I get a sense you're not from around here," said Junior.

"Green Bay."

"What are you doing over this way?" asked Helen.

"I'm actually on the home stretch of a several day journey to the dairying regions of the state. I left Green Bay last Wednesday. I started out by going south along the lakeshore and then cut over toward Madison. Then I went south and west and spent a couple of days in the Platteville area. Then I was on to Lacrosse before heading to Colby; and now I'm heading east."

"What in the world makes you want to take a trip like that?" responded Helen.

"Well, it's a along story. But basically, I grew up in Manitowoc County, lived out of state for several years and when I came back I noticed so many changes, especially as I drove the rural countryside. I wanted to learn how all the changes have been affecting diary farm families. I am a middle school teacher. I was lucky enough to secure a grant from a foundation. It's allowing me to pursue these kinds of issues."

"Sounds interesting. I'd like to hear more," said Junior.

"I've got an idea. Why don't you join us for lunch?" asked Helen. "We always come to the cemetery on a Thursday and then stop at the Roadside Cafe for their special. It's usually particularly good."

"You're sure I wouldn't be intruding?"

"Intruding? Not a chance. We'd love the company," said Junior.

"Then I'd be glad to," responded Michael. "Where exactly is this roadside cafe?"

"It's just up the road about a mile and a half. You cannot miss it. Better yet, why don't you just follow us?" suggested Junior.

Thursday Noon

About five minutes later Michael followed Boyd's blue Ford 150 into the gravel parking lot of a roadside cafe aptly called the "Roadside Cafe."

No sooner had they gotten in the door when a husky voice rang out: "Helen, Junior, we were hoping we'd see you here. Come, join us; and bring your friend, too."

It was Claude Jenkins. He was seated with his wife, Dorothea.

Helen turned and asked Michael, "Do you mind if we join them?"

"Of course not; the more the merrier," Michael responded as he, Helen and Junior made their way over to the Jenkins' table. When they arrived at the table, a waitress was already squeezing three additional place settings onto the four person table and calling out to the busboy: "Jimmy, can you bring another chair, please?"

Turning to Michael, Helen said: "Michel, these are our old neighbors, Claude and Dorothea Jenkins. They had the farm next to us for over forty years. Dorothea and Claude, this is Michael from Green Bay."

Junior, Helen and Michael sat down and Junior said to Michael: "Claude and Dorothea retired a few years ago and moved into a duplex in town. We sure miss them. Nothing like having good neighbors."

Claude interjected: "It's not been a few years. It is already almost ten. And we miss you and Helen too. Farm life is all I ever knew. Like they say: 'You can take the boy out of the country, but you can't take the country out of the boy.' But the work got to be too much for just the two of us. So we sold the cattle, the house, the barn and the outbuildings; but we still own 180 acres. We are renting the land to a guy whose milking over 1500 cows. He needs the cropland."

"I think I adjusted to life in town a little better than Claude," Dorothea said. "I've always been active at church and since we've been living in town, we seem to get called on to help out with whatever is going on. But I do not mind. Makes me feel like we're needed."

"Claude and Dorothea, we meet Michael at the cemetery," reported Junior.

Dorothea interrupted: "I assume you're still making your monthly visits to John and Boyd's graves?

"Yes we are," said Helen.

"Good for you, Helen, and good for you, Junior, for continuing to take your Mom," said Claude.

"I remember all too clearly the afternoon you told us that John had been killed. We had just taken over the farm from Claude's parents. It doesn't seem that so many years have passed," said Dorothea.

"I don't know how Boyd and I would have coped with it had it not been for friends like you," reported Helen.

"Well, that's what neighbors are for," said Dorothea.

"And they don't come any finer than you and Claude," said Helen. Her voice conveyed the gratitude she felt for these friends.

After a moment, Junior spoke: "As I was saying," said Junior, "We met Michael at the cemetery and we got to talking. He was telling us that he is spending several days traveling to the dairying regions of the state and seeking to discover how all the changes we have been experiencing are affecting us farmers. Sounded pretty fascinating to me."

"Me too, even though I'm no longer on the farm," said Claude.

Just then the waitress, Lucy, arrived with menus. "I don't think Claude and I need one," said Dorothea while Helen and Junior nodded in agreement indicating that they too, did not need menus. When Lucy looked toward Michael, he also declined a menu.

"Can I get you something to drink?" asked Lucy.

Each of the men opted for a bottle of "Spotted Cow" – a Wisconsin brewed specialty -- while both Helen and Dorothea ordered iced tea.

"I've been wanting to try a 'Spotted Cow' ever since I drove past the brewery in New Glarus last week," announced Michael.

"Well tell us, Michael, more about this project you're doing," requested Claude.

"How much do you want to hear?"

"As much as you want to tell us."

Encouraging Angels

With all eyes at the table focused on their guest, Michael began: "First of all, I need to tell you that I did not grow up on a dairy farm, but there were dairy farms all around us. We lived in the country and had a flock of chickens, but no cattle. This was in Manitowoc County. After I graduated from college, I went to Ohio for graduate school. That is where I met my wife, Elaine. I taught high school social studies for over twenty-five years in the Buckeye state and with my parents getting up in years, we moved back to Wisconsin a few years back. I have been teaching middle school social studies, while Elaine is a reading teacher. We're both employed by the Green Bay School District."

Lucy arrived with their drinks, placed them on the table and asked: "What can I get for you?"

They all decided on the day's special: Meatloaf served with mashed potatoes and gravy, a side of corn, plus a small side salad.

As Lucy took their order to the kitchen, Michael continued: "Anyhow, I was made aware of a sabbatical grant program for teachers. My grant proposal regarding the changes in the rural culture and their affects on the dairy farm family was approved for funding. And so I've been spending the past several days to research the topic, not in the library, but 'out on the field' you could say. I've been visiting with dairy farmers and others connected to farming in many parts of the state."

"And what are you finding out?" Claude inquired.

"More than I could have imagined."

"Like what?" asked Junior.

"Well, many things you are probably familiar with," said Michael.

"How about giving us a quick review? Maybe we can add to it," offered Junior.

"To start, there's the stagnant milk prices per hundred; farm couples having less children and when there are children, few of them want to take over the farm. Then there is the rising cost of machinery, competition from 'factory' farms, and despite all the technological advancements, the long number of working hours for farmers continues. There's just a lot of factors that make it harder and harder for farm families to keep their heads above water; and so most farm wives are working – at least part time – off the farm."

It was time for Helen to speak: "I remember years ago when we had to haul our milk to the cheese factory. Dad had an old beat up Chevy pickup and he could fit about eight cans in the back. Good thing the factory was just down the road, because I think we usually made two trips with each milking. But refrigeration – I'm referring to bulk tanks and the refrigerated trucks -- changed it all. Now our milk hauler comes once a day to pick up our milk and take it to the factory. And speaking of factories, there aren't nearly as many as there used to be."

"Excuse me for interrupting, Helen, but a fella at the Co-op in town was telling me the exact things earlier this morning."

Turning to Junior, Michael asked: "I'm sorry for not asking earlier, but do you live on the farm with your mom?"

"Yeah, I never married, and when dad died about ten years ago, it just made sense to stay on the home place. And it's worked out OK, hasn't it, mom?"

"Yes, Junior, I don't know what I'd do without you."

Just then Lucy arrived with a large tray holding five dinner plates each filled with meatloaf and mashed potatoes topped with gravy. Jimmy soon stood behind her. He was holding a tray containing the five side salads and small bowls of corn. After placing all the items in front of the group, Lucy secured four different types of salad dressing from a nearby table and placed the dressings on the table's only clear space. Then she asked Helen and Dorothea if they needed a refill of iced tea and the fellas if they were ready for another Spotted Cow. All politely refused.

Pointing at the small bowl in front of him, Junior remarked: "In another month or so, they'll still have corn for a side; but it will be fresh corn on the cob from a nearby farm."

"May I offer grace," asked Dorothea. No one answered, but her four dining companions all bowed their heads, as Dorothea thanked God for their friends, the food, the day, and their health. Helen and Junior concluded by making the "sign of the cross."

"Dig in" said Claude, "I think this is their best special. Although their Friday fish fry is pretty darn good, too."

"I agree," said Junior.

The meal was delicious and the five of them made "small talk" as they ate.

When they had finished their meals, Junior said: "Let's get back to Michael and listen to what else he's got for us."

Helen, Claude and Dorothea all nodded in agreement.

So Michael responded: "Like I said moments ago, more and more farm wives are employed off the farm. Not only does their income help to make ends meet, but they often carry the health insurance. Another thing I've been told more than once is how farmers are having fewer children. Thirty or forty years ago a half dozen or more kids was not uncommon. More kids meant more to help out with the farm work. And farm couples often kept having kids until at least one or more sons were born, hoping that one of them would take over the farm. Not any more; most of the farmers I've been meeting have only one or two children, three at tops."

Helen offered: "Being Catholic we know all about large families. Both Boyd and I came from large families. He had nine siblings; and I had three brothers and four sisters. Since birth control was frowned upon – or rather I should say prohibited -- many of our friends in our parish have quite a brood. Boyd and I stopped after John was born. I had a complicated pregnancy and Dr. Thomas advised me not to get pregnant again. So we started using birth control. Never let anybody know about it, especially not Father Joseph. At first we felt guilty about it; but then Dr. Thomas reassured us we were doing the right thing not only for my health, but for the well being of any child I might have conceived. I'm willing to bet that many younger people – even those who are Catholic – are using some form of birth control. It just makes sense with the cost of things."

Michael followed up: "Back when I was a student at Lakeland – the college I went to in rural Sheboygan County – I would often drive the country roads near the campus. If it was about four in the afternoon and I got behind a school bus, that bus would stop at just about every farm and drop off three or more kids. Now whenever I travel some of those same roads and I get behind a school bus, it often goes a mile or more between stops and very seldom drops off more than one or two children."

"Michael, I've got something to add about changes," offered Claude. "It's not directly about a change on the farm, but a change in small town and rural life. When I go to church, I look around and ask myself: 'Where are all our young people?' It used to be that our confirmation classes – a special class made up of young people in 8th or 9th grade – had a dozen or more kids. Now we offer confirmation every other year and are happy to have a class of four or five young people. Thirty years ago we had about 350 members and nearly one hundred children in Sunday School. We're down to less than 150 members and about thirty in Sunday School. We get about seventy-five or eighty folks for worship on Sunday morning and most of us are in our sixties or older. I keep wondering: What are we doing wrong? And what can we do to keep our young people? I'm not only talking about the teens and the younger children, I'm talking about their parents, too – folks in the thirties and forties. I've mentioned this to my friends who attend other churches, and it's the same story for them. But not only can we not keep our young people, we can't seem to keep our pastors, too. They come, stay a few years, and then move on. The church used to be at the center of many people's lives. Now it's lucky to be at the periphery. It seems like it's almost an afterthought."

"We Catholics are experiencing the same things," replied Junior.

Then, addressing Michael, Junior continued: "You probably sensed that no one was living in the St. Stanislaus' rectory. If so, you're right. There hasn't been a priest living in St. Stan's rectory for over fifteen years. We share a priest with three other parishes. And we sure don't seem to have nearly as many young men feeling called to the priesthood. I remember the day – again when couples were having lot of children – that it was kind of a badge of honor if one of their sons went into the priesthood. Doesn't seem to happen much anymore. Same was true with daughters. Parents hoped one or more of their daughters would enter some order and become a nun. Fact is: A lot of the priests in the rural area are coming from overseas.-- third world countries."

Michael replied: "I've been wondering about these changes in church life for quite a while. The church I was raised in – in rural Manitowoc County -- has seen its membership plummet over the last thirty or forty years. Same struggles: not enough younger adults and as a result, fewer children. And yes, shortly after youth are confirmed in 9th grade, they're only seen at Christmas and Easter. But then I looked at the church records, and I discovered it's been that way for quite a while. The young people of today are merely copying what their parents did thirty or more years ago.

"Elaine and I are now members of a church a little ways out of Green Bay. It had always been a rural church, but the city has been moving out in its direction, allowing our membership numbers to remain relatively steady. But I know that if it wasn't for the new housing in the neighborhood of the church, we'd be experiencing those same challenges. Still, the average age of our regular attendees is also around sixty, so many of us having been asking the same questions of what can we do to keep our young people and yes, how can we keep our ministers for more than three or four years? But then we came to realize something that seems to speak to these issues."

"What's that?" Dorothea and Claude asked simultaneously.

"Let me give you a little background... About a year after we became members of Bethel Church, the Chairperson of the Church Council asked Elaine and me if we would serve on the evangelism committee. I learned very quickly that the council was expecting that our committee would come up with ideas and plans to both get more members and to hang on to those we already have.

"Did you meet those expectations?" asked Claude.

"We learned that in regard to new residents in the area, we needed to be as welcoming as we can be. And that meant having members – not the pastor – invite these folks not only to worship, but to other activities of the church as well. And it also meant offering to pick them up for church events so they wouldn't have to show up by themselves. And once they were there, to introduce them to at least three other families. So far, numbers wise, it's been working out OK. We've gain about as many members as we lose due to job transfers, deaths, and young people moving away. But I've got to admit – I don't like to get caught up in a numbers game. It seems like there's much more that we need to be about.

"It's when we – that is, our committee -- started talking about what we can do to 'keep' our young people that we had a breakthrough. Jennifer Wesson, one of our committee members whose oldest son had just finished college and whose daughter was just starting college at Carroll down in Waukesha said, 'Chad just graduated from Lawrence and he's landed a job in Milwaukee, and there's a good chance when our Amy is through, she'll be living somewhere other than Green Bay. We've got to quit thinking we're doing something wrong and that we need to be doing something so that we can stop losing our young people.'

"She continued, 'All of us here are parents. And as much as we would like to keep our children close to us, we know we can't hold on to them forever. They will fly from the nest. We can't stop that. And I honestly think we do not want to strop that. But what we can do is provide them with all we can -- and I'm not talking things like money -- but things like good values – kindness, honesty, and a good work ethic, so that when they leave, they will take those good things with them.'

"By this time Jennifer had everyone's attention. She went on: 'Maybe that's what we need to be doing with our young people. Not worrying about how we can keep them. For the truth is, we can't. But concentrate on how we can prepare them morally and spiritually so that when they do leave us, when they take their wings and fly, they'll be able to plant some strong roots wherever they land.'

"When Jennifer finished speaking you could have heard a pin drop. We all knew she was on to something.

"Then Elaine added: 'When our Sarah was born we found a poster and put it up our study. It said that parents are to give their children roots and wings. What you're saying, Jennifer, sounds a lot like that. You're absolutely right: We can't prevent our children from leaving. It's going to happen. Let's face it: Young people grow up and they go away for school or to find work. We can't hang on to them.'

"And then we had that 'Aha!' moment as Dick Jaegger, one of the committee's quieter members spoke what I 'd like to think we were all thinking: 'Maybe we're

Encouraging Angels

asking the wrong question. Instead of beating our heads against the wall and wondering what we doing wrong and what we can do to keep our young people, we need to be focusing on how can we equip them and send them out. Maybe our job is not to keep them, but to send them. Send them out. Isn't that what Jesus did? He sent out his disciples. Maybe the best thing we can do is prepare them, teach them, encourage them, so that when they do go out – they can take what they have leaned and experienced here and share that with others in some other church in some other place. It will be as if we are sending out missionaries. And I might add, hopefully other churches will be doing the same thing with their young people, so that when they leave – if one or more of them find their way to Green Bay – maybe they can become a part of our congregation, enriching our lives, just as we have sent out our young people to enrich the lives of others. Maybe that's part of our call to be evangelists who share the good news of Jesus, and one of the best things we can do as an evangelism committee.'

"I need to tell you, it was if a whole new spirit filled the air. I'd like to think of it as the Holy Spirit filling us with a new understanding as to what we needed to be about as a congregation: preparing our young people so well and giving them such a positive faith experience that when they move away from us, they do so filled with the knowledge of the love and grace of God; so that they cannot help but want to get plugged into another church whenever they find themselves, and then share that good news with others.

"Not only was our way of thinking transformed, but when we presented our theory – if we can call it that – the whole council bought into it; and we intentionally began a campaign that proclaimed: 'We're not losing them; were sending them!'"

"How is it going?" asked Dorothea.

"It's a work in progress. Maybe I shouldn't call it a 'work,' but rather a sacred responsibility that never ends."

"It sounds to me like you're really on to something. I'm going to share this with our outreach committee," said Dorothea.

Then she asked: "But what about the other dilemma that many of us face? Our inability to keep a pastor for more than three or four years; so that we are referred to as 'a stepping stone' for a pastor on their way to what is usually a larger church where they receive greater compensation. And the reason I am asking that is because of what's happened to us at

First Presbyterian. We're searching once again for a new pastor. Pastor Reed came to us four years ago – fresh out of seminary, loaded with wonderful ideas and filled with enthusiasm. He's done an excellent job and has been well received. But just like all the other good ones, he was called to a larger and I assume more prestigious church. He and his wife are moving to Eau Claire next month."

"I'm sorry to hear that. I know last time we saw you, you spoke so highly of him," said Helen to her friend.

Michael jumped in: "If I may, funny thing happened. As our committee was talking about sending out our young people, our conversation took a slight turn. Our thoughts concerning our youth somehow led us to some considerations regarding pastors, and we started talking about how can we keep our pastors for a longer time.

"Again it was Dick who spoke up: 'Maybe it's just like our young people and maybe were asking the wrong question. It's not how can we keep them, but what can we do with them while we have them. Let me explain what I mean: Most smaller or rural congregations are often served by a pastor right out of seminary. Usually it is their first call. Well, I believe that the seminary doesn't teach a pastor all he or she needs to know about being a pastor. Much of that comes with experience. And it is their first call that can provide that experience. I once heard that a pastor's first call makes them or breaks them, and we've all heard those horror stories where pastor's first call was so rough on him or her that he or she left the ministry after their first appointment or call. I'd like to think our job is to help 'make' them.'

"Then Elaine responded: 'So what you are saying is that even if a pastor leaves after only a few years, the congregation can still feel good about themselves if they have helped that pastor to grow and helped that pastor identify his or her strengths as well as areas that may still need improvement.'"

"Dick responded: 'That's exactly what I'm saying. Again the small town or rural congregation may not keep their pastor for an extended time, but they have the opportunity to send out the pastor. And having helped to shape him or her, that pastor goes out from them – if I may say – a better pastor. And such training by that congregation becomes their gift to the wider church. I think the small town or rural church may be uniquely positioned to do this.'"

"Michael, you've got me thinking," said Claude. "I think when we focus on KEEPING rather than SENDING, we lose a sense of our real mission – our purpose, if you will -- and we begin to fall into a survival mode rather than a mission mode. Remember what is called the 'Great Commission' offered by Jesus at the end of Matthew's gospel. He said we are to go and make disciples of all nations, baptizing them in the name of God – Father, son and Holy Spirit -- and teaching them to observe all that he had taught them. And in Acts, just before Jesus ascends, he gives his followers similar instructions when he said: 'You shall be my witnesses in Jerusalem and Judea, in Samaria and to the ends of the earth.' It seems to me that the emphasis in these two sets of final words of Jesus is not about keeping, but about sending, going out and sharing – sharing the good news, the gospel. It seems to me that if we do this sending out of our young people and our pastors, we will be doing not only a great service to the wider church, but we'll also be faithfully following those last instructions that Jesus gave to his first followers."

"Precisely!" agreed Michael. "The sending in both of these cases becomes a much more positive endeavor than a church simply worrying about holding on to either its young people or its pastors. The sending is really a gift that certainly all congregations can do; but again, it seems that the small town or rural church may be best positioned to offer. And what a wonderful gift it can be. Certainly, the congregation who does such sending has every right to feel good about what they are doing."

"Mind if I share this with our search and call committee?" asked Dorothea.

"No; not at all," responded Michael. "These realizations have done wonders for the mood and climate of Bethel Church. Instead of feeling that 'we must be doing something wrong,' we've found a whole new focus and we feel we're doing something right. We're sending instead of keeping and it's been pretty exciting."

"Well, I hate to be a party-pooper," said Claude, "but Dorothea and I have an appointment with our financial adviser at the bank at 1:30, so we're going to have to shove off."

"Helen and Junior, it's always good to see you, and thank you for bringing Michael. And yes, give our greetings to the old neighborhood," added Dorothea.

"It's always good to spend time with you, Dorothea and Claude," said Helen.

"Remember, we stop here for lunch every month after going to the cemetery," said Junior in such a way as to indicate that he was hoping that he and his mom would run into Claude and Dorothea once again at the Roadside Cafe. "And stop out at the farm anytime."

"And remember, you're always welcome to come and see us at our duplex," said Dorothea. "And so long to you, Michael. Much success in your travels."

Michael reached out to shake the hands of his lunch mates and made his way to the cash register to pay his check.

As he turned toward the door, he looked over at the table and waved to the four friends. His heart was warmed by the way he imagined they had supported each other through the ups and downs of their life experiences.

Thursday Afternoon

Proceeding east, Michael immediately noticed a sign advertising the Wisconsin Valley Fair. The sign said: "Since 1869." Michael was amazed. "This fair has been occurring annually for well over a century and a half and it's happening in Wausau this weekend," Michael said as he read the sign. "I think that's worth a stop."

County fairs have been an annual tradition in many rural areas. Not only was Michael pleased to see that this tradition continues, he also assumed that stopping at the fair would offer yet another setting to visit with folks connected to dairy farming. He decided that when he arrived in Wausau, he'd find a motel for the night and then check out the fair.

Michael joined State Highway 29 just west of Wausau and proceeded to the Rib Mountain exit. As he pulled off the highway he noticed an assortment of motels. He opted for the Sky View Inn, a 60's style establishment that offered wonderful views of the mountain. He checked in shortly after 2 P.M. Finding his room, he thought he'd take a nap before heading for the fairgrounds.

Sleep came rather easily. It's a good thing he had set his alarm for 4:30. He awoke, found his truck keys and his room key and set out for the fairgrounds.

Thursday Evening

Michael arrived at the fair just after 5 P.M. After pulling his pickup into a large field designated for parking, he walked to the front gate and paid his admission. Taking a few steps further, he noticed a sign listing the events of the day. Included were swine, diary cattle, calf and canned food judging in the morning and harness racing in the afternoon. The midway – with its carnival rides, games and food stands would be open from 11 A.M. to 9 P.M. Then his eye caught one other event on the day's schedule: a 4-H speaking contest at 7 P.M. This was to occur in Exposition Building A that was located just inside the main gate. Michael decided he would try to take this in. But first, he'd walk through the main cattle barn, check out the midway and grab some food at one of the food stands.

Michael's first stop was the barn housing the diary cows. He noticed various colored ribbons displayed on the large wooden beams just above the cattle. Having been judged earlier in the day, there were several blue ribbons, even more red ones and some were white. Years earlier Michael had learned that the color of ribbon did not necessarily represent first, second or third place, but rather a level of achievement. A blue ribbon means that the exhibit is outstanding on all standards. A red ribbon indicates that it exceeds minimum standards, but still needs minor improvements. And the exhibits bearing white ribbons meet minimum standards, but need improvement. As Michael looked at the cattle, he felt they all seemed worthy of a blue ribbon. But then he admitted he did not know "the standards." He assumed that being a judge required an extremely trained and critical eye to know what separated a blue ribbon cow from a red ribbon one, and a red one from a white one.

Then he saw one stall sporting a large purple ribbon. As he drew closer he realized this was the grand champion milk cow. Sitting on a hay bale near the cow was a girl whom Michael thought was about 14 or 15.

Michael said to her: "That sure is an attractive milk cow."

The girl stood up, patted her cow on her back and said: "Lulu has been my 4-H project this past year, but I've raised her since her birth four years ago." Although Michael knew nothing about judging cattle, he sensed something special about this particular milk cow. Maybe it was her posture, her cleanliness, or just the way she interacted with her caregiver. He could see why Lulu had been awarded he purple ribbon as the top exhibit in the category.

"Well, keep up the good work," Michael said to the teen. "She sure is a beautiful animal."

After leaving the cattle barn Michael headed for the midway. The carnival rides were the usual Tilt-A-Wheel, Scrambler, Ferris Wheel and others. Then there were games of chance offering prizes ranging from small trinkets to the coveted large stuffed animals. Scattered throughout the midway were trailers selling the traditional carnival foods, such as corn dogs, elephant ears and cotton candy. Then there was a row of food tents, all operated by area churches an civic organizations. Each seemed to offer their own specialty. Walking among the tents, Michael took inventory: The Lion's Club sold fresh fried cheese curds, and First Methodist Church squeezed lemons for their refreshing lemonade. The Farm Bureau's specialty was cream puffs. St. Christopher Church offered fried fish sandwiches, along with french fries and soda. The V.F.W. had chicken wings, and the Optimists specialized in cheese sandwiches. The sign at the entrance to the Optimists' tent proudly announced: "We use only cheese from nearby factories." The Presbyterian Church was grilling fresh brats, the United Church of Christ was serving hot dogs and hamburgers, and the Lutheran Church's specialties were various pies and ice cream.

The aroma wafting from the food tents seemed to intensify Michael's appetite and soon he was deliberating a stop at one of the food tents. Since it was almost Friday, and because he was grateful to Roman Catholicism for one of Wisconsin's best food traditions – the Friday fish fry -- he decided he would eat at the St. Christopher food tent. He walked to the counter and ordered the fish combo: a fried fish sandwich, fries and a Coke, all for seven bucks.

The volunteer behind the counter received Michael's order and encouraged Michael to sit at one of the card tables located just to the right of the food service counter. "One of our crew will deliver your order in just a minute," said the order taker.

As was often true during his time on the road, Michael was hungrier than he thought. He finished his fish combo very quickly.

As he was taking his last bite, one of the volunteers from St. Christopher's who was wearing a name tag with the name Edwin printed on it, came over to Michael's table and said: "Mind if I pull up a chair?"

Michael said: "No. By all means, have a seat. You look like you could use a break. I bet you've been at this all afternoon."

The fella identified himself as Edwin Koudelka, and said he was a long time member of St. Christopher's. He asked Michael: "I don't believe we've ever met. Are you a member of our parish?"

"No," said Michael. "Just passing through Wausau on my way back home to Green Bay."

"Well then it's probably safe for me to say: I don't know how much longer we'll be able to operate this food tent. Harder and harder each year to get volunteers. Father Jerome has to beg – starting right after Easter – to secure helpers. It's been a tradition for over sixty years to serve the fish sandwiches at the fair. And it usually brings in about ten grand to the parish annually. The work really isn't all that hard, once have the volunteers. And we have a lot of fun doing it. I always say that I do it -- not for the money we raise -- but for the fellowship we all enjoy; and seeing all the people who stop by our tent."

"You say that St. Christopher's has been operating this tent for over sixty years?"

"Yes," replied Edwin.

"And you hope to do it again next year, provided you have sufficient volunteers?" inquired Michael.

"Of course." Edwin answered. "The money we raise is used to help support some pretty vital ministries, including our food bank, emergency housing, and a couple of scholarships for our young people."

"Mind if I share an idea that might help recruit some volunteers?" asked Michael.

"Not at all. What's your idea? You've got my undivided attention until I have to go back to work."

"Well next year about six weeks or two months before fair time, ask Father – your priest – if you can make an announcement at mass. And instead of saying we need such and such a number of volunteers for the tent, tell them what it has meant for you to have been a volunteer over the years. Build it up as an opportunity for fellowship and friendship; not just as a money-making enterprise. If you announce what you just told me of what it means to you – and say it with the same passion you just had while speaking to me, I bet you'll get some takers. Also, if you haven't done so, make a plea to the newer members of the parish, informing them that working at the food tent is an opportunity to meet and get to know some of the more established members of the parish. And have a couple of college students who have been recipients of your scholarships tell your parish how that support has helped them; in fact, they should volunteer since they have benefited."

"Interesting approach. Do you think it will work?" asked Edwin.

"Doesn't hurt trying. You'll still have some folks who will want to concentrate on the money-making aspect of it; but I think if you appeal to the mission side of the food tent tradition, you'll get more help. I read somewhere that younger people will volunteer for something if they know exactly what they are volunteering for, the length of their commitment, and if what they are volunteering for has a good purpose. They want to feel they're really making a contribution to something important. It's obvious you feel that way. And from what you told me about where the proceeds go – they are all noble causes -- I think you'll find some folks buying into it and volunteering." replied Michael.

"I like your ideas. I'll share them with some of our seasoned veterans around here. And when I go home tonight, I'm going to write them down and put them in my top dresser drawer; then I'm have them for next spring when we start our planning for next year.

"Looks like we're getting quite a crowd again," Edwin observed, as he noticed a group that was gathering to place their orders. "I better get back to my post. Nice to visit with you, Michael, and thanks for the ideas."

After Edwin stood up and returned to his position at the french fryer, Michael thought: That's a common dilemma for so many organizations and churches – finding willing volunteers. Volunteerism isn't what it used to be – another change from thirty, forty years ago. I guess we need to be open to new approaches for securing volunteers. I do know that once folks volunteer and find themselves working together on some worthy project, they're usually glad they did.

Checking his watch, it was almost 6:30 P.M. Michael decided to take off for Exposition Building A, the location of the speech contest. He recalled it was near the main entrance to the fair. The building was about a ten minute walk through the crowded midway and when he arrived, he was handed a printed program listing the ten contestants and the particular 4-H Club they were representing. He noted that the participants had to have competed their freshman year of high school. Eligibility ceased at the end of the summer following their graduation from high school. He also learned that each speech was to be between five and seven minutes in length and each participant was required to speak on one – and only one -- of the H's in 4-H pledge. It was up to each speaker to decide whether he or she wanted to speak on head, hands, heart or health. The choice was theirs.

"This sounds interesting," Michael said in a soft voice to no one in particular.

Michael peered toward the area of the pavilion where the contest was to be held. There appeared to be enough seating for an audience of about one hundred; and when Michael arrived – about twenty minutes before the start of the event -- only about twenty seats were occupied. He noticed four or five young people whom he assumed were some of the contestants. Each was seated close to one or two adults; their parents, Michael thought.

Michael decided to use the rest room before the contest started. He found a men's room in the Administration Building just across the walkway from the Exposition Building. As he entered he immediately saw a youth leaning over one of the four sinks. Since the fella was wearing dress slacks and shirt and a tie, Michael assumed that the lad – about fifteen or sixteen -- was one of the participants in the speech contest. As Michael washed his hands in a nearby sink, he looked over to the youth and asked:

Encouraging Angels

"Nervous?"

"Yes," and then after belching, added: "I think I might throw up."

"How about taking three deep breaths?"

"I'll try."

The fella did and he seemed to calm a bit.

"There you go. Feel any better?" Michael asked.

"I don't feel I'm going to upchuck anymore, but I don't ever remember being so nervous in my entire life."

"You're in the speech contest, I bet."

"How'd you know?"

"Look in the mirror. What teenager would come to the fair wearing dress slacks, and shirt and tie. Plus, I read the sign that says: '4-H speech contest at 7 P.M. Exposition Building A.'"

Michael continued: "Let me ask you a question...

Michael paused and the young fella assumed Michael was going to ask for his name.

Encouraging Angels

"Tanner."

"Tanner, let me ask you a question: Do you think you wrote a good speech?"

"Yes, I think I did the best I could."

"Then you've got nothing to worry about, do you?" encouraged Michael.

"Well, I'd just like to get this over with," said Tanner.

"You sound exactly like someone I used to know," replied Michael.

"Who's that?"

"Me, when I was about your age, Tanner."

"Really. How's that?" asked Tanner.

"We'll, whenever I had to give a speech, especially the speeches we had to give in English class, I'd kind of freak out, too. I'd write a pretty good speech and then I got so nervous when it was time to give it, I just wanted to present it and sit down, and be glad it was all over."

Michael had Tanner's full attention.

So Michael went on: "But then someone once told me that being nervous means you're well prepared. And I have a strong hunch that you are well prepared."

"Yes, I spent plenty of time with my speech and I like what I've written."

"Good. Sounds like you've prepared a speech you can be proud of. Now let me tell you something else I learned. One day I thought to myself that if the speech I wrote is good, I shouldn't blow it in the presentation. After all, if it is well written, I should be proud to present it. That didn't take away all the nervousness at once, but over time it did. I even started entering some speech contests -- like you -- to keep practicing.

"You see, I always wanted to be a teacher and I knew that being a teacher meant standing up in front of twenty to twenty-five students every day and speaking to them. I knew if that was my dream, I needed to keep working out my nervousness; and given time, I got the nervousness under control.

"There's one more thing I learned and still tell myself whenever I give a speech. Although there may be twenty or thirty or a hundred people in the audience, it's really as if you are speaking to one person at a time; the others are just happening to be listening in to the conversation. So look to one person for a little while like you are speaking only to him; then find another and speak to her for a while, and in the end it will be like you've spoken to ten or fifteen different people in the audience, but it's always been like a one on one conversation."

"Does it work?" asked Tanner."

"It has for me, and it allows good eye contact; and that's always something the judges are watching for."

"So did you end up becoming a teacher?"

"I did. I'm a middle school social studies teacher in Green Bay. My name, by the way, is Michael – Michael Lattimore."

"Mr. Lattimore, don't tell me; you're not one of the judges, are you? Contestants are not supposed to have any conversations with the judges before the contest."

"No, don't worry Tanner. I'm not one of the judges. I'm just interested in what kids are doing."

Tanner turned and as he walked toward the door, he said to Michael: "Mr. Lattimore, nice that you took the time to talk with me. Thank you. I better get back in there. It's getting close to seven. And my folks should have arrived by now."

"There's just one more thing Tanner," Michael said: "I'm guessing nobody made you enter this speech contest. Am I right?"

"You're right. When I heard what the topics were that we could speak about, I felt I could write a pretty good speech."

"You're already taking a first big step in overcoming your fears; you're putting yourself out there. So just go and give it your best shot," said Michael.

Tanner headed back across the gravel lane between the rest rooms and thee exposition building. As he entered the building he spotted his parents and went to sit with them. Michael paused for a further moment in the restroom. He had yet to remove some ketchup that had somehow ended up on his shirt. After some rigorous scrubbing, the shirt was presentable and he returned to the exposition building. He took a seat in the last row. He was glad to see that most of the folding chairs were now occupied.

Michael turned to his brochure again and noted that there were to be three judges. He looked to the front

Encouraging Angels

where he thought they would be located, but there was only one chair behind the podium. Then he noticed three folks among the crowd – one near the front on the left, one in almost the very center and one in the back on the right -- who were holding clipboards along with steno pads. He assumed they were the judges.

A moment later a very classy woman about fifty years of age strode to the front. Most of the folks in attendance seemed to recognize her. As she took her place behind the podium, she identified herself:

"Good evening. I'm Marilyn Baxter. Most of you know me as your circuit judge. Tonight, however, I am doing no judging. That's the job of three others seated among you who will be introduced after all the speeches have been given. I have been asked by the area 4-H leadership to serve as tonight's host and to introduce our speakers. And so instead of hearing a set of 'your honors,' this evening, it is 'my honor' and privilege to 'preside' – if I may use the term – over this evening's gathering.

"As we begin this evening I invite us to stand and join together in reciting the 4-H pledge. For those of you who have not memorized it, the pledge is found on the back of your brochure."

All in attendance stood and spoke in unison: "I pledge my head to clearer thinking, my heart for greater loyalty, my hands to larger service, and my health to better living for my club, my community, my country and my world."

After the group was seated, Ms. Baxter went on: "I want to remind you that rather than one common theme addressed by all the participants, each speaker's presentation will focus on one of the four principles of the pledge we just spoke. Again they include: 'My head to clearer thinking,' 'my heart for greater loyalty,' 'my hands to larger service,' and 'my health to better living.' Each speaker's presentation will be between five and seven minutes in length. Our judges will be looking at how well our participants address the aspect of the pledge that they have chosen to base their remarks. Judging will be also be based on style and delivery. There will be ten speakers. Each contestant represents a different 4-H Club from Marathon County. To determine the order of our speakers, a different name appears on each of ten index cards that have been placed in this basket."

Ms. Baxter held up a small wicker basket containing the cards with the names of the contestants.

"I will draw one name and that young person will present his or her speech. After that speech is completed and the judges have had a moment to finish their evaluation, I will draw a second name and that young person will address us. We will continue in this manner until all ten of our contestants have delivered their speeches. After the last speech has been given we will take a ten minute break during which time the judges will do their final tabulations. Then we will come back from recess and the judges will announce the top thee finishers.

"So how about we get started?"

All in the audience appeared to take a deep breath. Then Ms. Baxter reached in the basket, pulled out the first card and announced: "Joy Carter. Joy is the representative from the Mink Creek Club."

Joy, a freckle-faced redhead Michael thought to be about fourteen, approached the podium, giggled a bit, cleared her throat and began. She focused on using "her hands for larger service." Joy noted how hands can be used to reach out to others in compassionate and caring ways. She spoke about hands being used in cooking, cleaning, and farm work ranging from milking cows to driving a tractor. Then she spoke about hands she would never forget – the hands of her late grandmother who had taught her how to crochet and knit. Her speech was informative and heart-felt, and Michael knew that with nine additional speeches, the judges did not have an easy task. He even told himself that he was glad he was not one of the judges.

One by one Ms. Baxter drew names from the wicker basket and one by one the youth offered their speeches. On her seventh draw, she pulled out the index card bearing the name: Tanner Sullivan of the Eager Beaver 4-H Club. Michael perked up. As Tanner walked to the podium, Michael's heart began to race. He thought to himself: I can't believe how I've gotten so emotionally invested in this contest.

Tanner began his speech. He immediately caught the attention of his listeners with a question: "Do you know that every time you encourage someone, you put heart into them? For the word encourage comes from two early Greek words – 'en' and 'cor' – meaning 'in' and 'heart.' So that whenever you encourage someone, your action or your words puts heart into them."

Michael quickly realized that Tanner was focusing on the section of the pledge that states: "My heart to greater loyalty." Michael whispered to himself: "And what a good way to start a speech: By asking a question, he has the audience immediately involved."

Tanner continued: "Obviously when I say the word 'heart' – I'm not referring to the muscle that consists of chambers and valves that pumps our blood. Rather, I am defining the heart as the seat of our emotions."

Was Tanner nervous? Yes, but it did not distract from his presentation. He was controlled and direct in his delivery, and Michael could see him zeroing in our various faces in the audience. He spoke clearly and with confidence.

Tanner drew several nods of approval when he said: "When you do something with heart, you are passionate about it. You will give it everything you've got. Doing something with heart means putting forth your best effort. And when you give someone your heart, you are giving that person your all. That's what commitment and loyalty are all about."

Tanner went on to mention a scene from his favorite movie. Called "The Replacements," the film centered around a football team that was comprised of replacement players. "Why we they referred to as 'replacement players?'" Tanner asked, and then he answered: "Because the regular players were on strike." Then Tanner made his point: "When the team's coach was asked by a reporter what it would take to win, the coach tapped his chest with a rolled up paper that contained his game plan and said, 'Heart; it will take heart.'

Tanner continued to make his point: "Later on in the movie the coach was asked by another reporter if he would rather have his star quarterback who was no longer on strike lead the team or have the replacement quarterback – a fella named Falco – assume the leadership role, the coach replied: 'Falco.' When the reporter asked: 'Why Falco?' the coach responded: 'Heart; Falco plays with heart.'"

Tanner's comments regarding "heart" caused Michael to recall a sermon delivered by his pastor on a recent Sunday. The sermon was based on the gospel story where Jesus is walking on the water and he is approaching his frightened disciples who are aboard a boat. The first thing Jesus said to his companions was a simple two word imperative: "Take heart." Michael remembered that his pastor said: "Jesus was encouraging his disciples, putting heart into them."

Tanner finished and returned to his seat amid the polite applause that each of the contestants had been receiving. Along the way Tanner caught Michael's eye and thy nodded to each other. Tanner sensed that Michael's nod was a "one of approval"-- one that indicated that he had done a good job. Tanner's assumption was correct. Michael was proud of

Encouraging Angels

Tanner and pleased that he spoke quite eloquently and convincingly. His content was good; and his presentation demonstrated confidence, clarity, passion, good volume and certainly good eye contact.

Michael settled back to hear the remaining three contestants. A little over an hour after Ms. Baxter had introduced Joy Carter, the last of the ten contestants finished his speech. Two of the ten contestants had addressed the HEAD theme, four spoke about the HEART, three focused on HANDS, and one on HEALTH. Michael, who had not been a 4-H member as a youth, felt he had learned a good deal about 4-H and was inspired by the young people who had all spoken so well. It was time for that brief break Ms. Baxter had mentioned earlier.

The Marathon County Farm Bureau had supplied several trays loaded with prize-winning cheeses from area factories. Along with cheddar, muenster, brick, and of course Colby, four Dairy Princesses representing various communities in the county served coffee, milk and iced tea. Some of the audience went to the rear of the room to sample the goodies.

Meanwhile the contestants were being congratulated by not only their family members, but by the families of the other contestants as well. And almost all contestants were either "high-fiving" or patting each other on their backs. It was a wonderful scene of good sportsmanship and camaraderie that Michael knew that he would remember for a very long time. Although they had been competitors moments earlier, Michael sensed there was much more to this event than competition. He got the distinct feeling that the ten young people were co-participants in a common effort – an effort that allowed the 4-H motto to "come alive" in a special way.

Soon, Ms. Baxter returned to the podium and invited the attendees and speakers back to their seats. Everyone returned quickly, anxious to learn the results.

"Before we hear the results," said Ms. Baxter, "I want to introduce our evening's judges, and as I do so, I ask that they please come forward and stand beside me. First we have Dr. Janet Sewell; she is a speech and dramatic arts professor at the University of Wisconsin in Stevens Point."

Dr. Sewell stood and approached the front as the crowd offered their polite applause.

"Next is Bradley Jamison. He is an Agriculture and Industrial Arts Teacher from Medford."

Again, polite applause occurred as Bradley walked forward.

"And our third judge is Dexter Bartholomew. Dexter is the associate editor of 'Hoard's Dairyman.'" Dexter walked forward."

Again, applause filled the air as Dexter joined his fellow judges.

"Have you finalized your decisions," Ms. Baxter inquired?

"We have," all three judges responded in unison.

"Well then, let me step aside. I believe you've chosen Mr. Jamison to be your spokesperson."

Bradley Jamison approached the podium and began to speak: "On behalf of Dr. Sewell, Mr. Bartholomew and myself, we want to thank all ten participants, their families who supported them and the clubs they represent. Each young person did a fine job and each can be proud of what they've prepared and now presented. It was a little tricky for us to judge since not all spoke on the same topic. But we have to admit that the four major themes of head, heart, hands, and health proved to be enlightening to all of us. We enjoyed all ten presentations. However, the speeches from three of our participants stood out for us, and we want to recognize these three as our third, second and first place prize winners.

"And so, in third place: Speaking on the HEAD theme – Carly Johnston.

"Carly, will you come forward an receive your third place award from Ms. Baxter?"

Carly, a tall girl with short blond hair who Michael thought was about sixteen walked forward flashing a wide smile. The audience applauded as she was handed a small plaque indicating her third place finish.

"In second place, speaking on the HEART theme – Tanner Sullivan. Please come up, Tanner."

Tanner stood, looked toward Michael and flashed him a thumbs up sign which Michael reciprocated. Then he turned and walked to the front to receive his second place plaque from Ms. Baxter. The applause grew a little louder.

"And our first place prize winner, speaking on the HANDS theme – Maggie Dolski. Maggie, please come forward and receive your award."

Maggie, appearing to be one of the older of the ten participants, stepped up to accept the first place award. The greatest applause had been reserved for her.

Michael thought Maggie's speech was well-crafted and presented with both poise and confidence.

She began not by speaking, but by holding her hands about a foot from her face and staring at them for a number of seconds. Then she said: "Hands. My hands. When I look at my hands I see my mother's hands and when I look at my mom's hands, I see Gramma Beatrice's hands. Mom's appear like Gramma's and mine are beginning to look like Mom's."

Maggie had gone on to speak about these women's hands and the work they had accomplished: working in the garden, canning vegetables, milking cows, kneading bread and hanging the wash on the line. She mentioned that about their hands were gentle whenever they touched her fevered forehead, and were calming whenever she was frightened. Maggie continued: "Their hands not only completed jobs or duties, but they were also expressions of their love as they made their contributions to others. For their hands were also used to knit blankets, sew clothes and crochet hats and scarves to those in need. I also know their hands also gently caressed me as an infant, were at work as they brushed my hair, gripped me when I crossed the road, and held me when I felt my heart was broken."

She had concluded by saying: "In the 21st century I will probably not do all the same things my mother and grandmother did with their hands. I hope to go to college and pursue a degree in nursing. Again, I don't know if I will use my hands in all the same ways my mother and grandmother did, but as a nurse, I hope I will reach out with similar care and compassion to those entrusted to my care."

Maggie had delivered a very good speech. She certainly spoke to the theme: "My hands to greater service." Michael felt that Maggie was well deserving of the first place prize, and that the judges had done a fine job with their responsibility.

Ms. Baxter announced that Maggie would be Marathon County's representative in the state level competition that would occur at the state fair in Milwaukee in early August. Ms. Baxter added: "And, if for some reason Maggie is not able to participate, Tanner – who finished in second place this evening -- will take her place."

With the awards presented, Ms. Baxter thanked everyone for coming. She thanked the participants and the judges and announced that she hoped that next year's contest would be as successful as this year's. Then she bid everyone a good evening. Again there was an applause, followed by part of the audience proceeding toward the exit. Others stood and visited in small groups.

Tanner motioned for Michael to come over and join him and his parents. On the way Michael walked past Carly. He paused to congratulate her for her third place finish. When Michael reached Tanner and his family, Tanner said to Michael: "I want you to meet my mom and dad, Shirley and George. Mom and dad this is Mr. Lattimore."

After they greeted one another, George said to Michael: "I want to thank your for what you did for our son. He always gets so nervous before things like this. He told us just before the contest began how you helped to calm him down; and how you gave him some pointers on how he could present his speech. Obviously, they worked well. We just want to say how much we appreciate what you did."

Michael replied: "I just happened to be in the right place at the right time. I thought Tanner did an excellent job."

Tanner interjected: "I was still a little nervous, but I tried to follow your suggestions and I think they really helped. Mr. Lattimore, you're an example of what I was talking about. You encouraged me and 'put heart' into me. Needless to say, that helped with my presentation."

Shirley added: "Mr. Lattimore..."

Michael interrupted: "Please call me Michael."

"Michael, Tanner said you're a teacher from Green Bay. I bet you're a darn good one and that the kids are glad to have you."

Michael responded: "I love teaching; but you'd have to ask my students if I'm any good at it."

George asked: "Do you mind me asking, what brings you over here to our fair?"

Michael responded: "Since it's getting late, I'll give you the short version. I'm actually on a sabbatical journey. I am looking at dairy farming around the state and trying to determine how all the changes that continue to take place are affecting dairy farm families. I actually left Green Bay over a week ago and I am on the home stretch. I noticed the sign a couple of miles back up the road advertising the fair, and I thought: Here's another opportunity to meet and speak with folks associated with farming."

Shirley said, "I'm sorry to interrupt, but we promised to take Tanner for some ice cream at our church's food tent after the contest. They're supposed to be open until 9. If we hurry, we can get there before they shut down for the night. Would you care to join us, Michael?"

"Sure, thank you; I never miss a chance for ice cream."

Shirley and George, Tanner and Michael walked toward the St. Paul Lutheran ice cream and pie tent. Michael noticed that the Sullivans said "Hello" to nearly half the persons they passed en route. As the four neared the tent, a cute girl about Tanner's age called out from behind the serving counter: "Tanner, how'd you do?"

"Second place," replied Tanner.

"Good job; I'm proud of you, Tanner," said the smiling teen.

"That's Jordan Bowman. She and Tanner have been good friends since first grade. They've always been in the same class at school and the same Sunday School class at church," reported Shirley to Michael.

Tanner, his mom and dad, and Michael stepped up to the counter a few minutes before 9 and placed their order: Tanner ordered two scoops of chocolate; his mom had a scoop of strawberry. George and Michael each had two scoops – one vanilla and the other chocolate.

They sat down at one of the folding tables that had been set up under the large tent. Two minutes later Jordan appeared with their treats. Then Michael's conversation with the Sullivans continued.

Michael asked George and Shirley if they were involved in dairy farming.

"Yes, but indirectly," George said. "I'm a loan officer at the bank in Marathon. Most of my clients are farmers, a few grain farmers, but mostly dairy farmers. Some of them think they must expand – gather a larger herd and more crop land -- to make a go of it. And it works for some. But for others, it just doesn't work out. The number of foreclosures keeps growing. And I feel terrible when that happens. In many cases, I approved their loans. Truth is, when it's your friends and folks you've known all your life, and you know they're extremely hard workers, it's hard not to approve their loan requests. And it's even harder if they default.'"

"I can only imagine the difficult position you often find yourself," replied Michael.

"And I've been with the school district for almost twenty years. No; I'm not a teacher. I work in the office and have been the district secretary for the past five years," said Shirley.

"So, you run the district," Michael said with a tone of voice indicating he was only partly kidding. Then he added: "I know that school secretaries are often the cog in the whole operation; and without a good district secretary, any smooth functioning of the school or district is put in jeopardy."

"Well, thank you for considering my position so important. I wish everyone in our district shared your estimation."

"Where are you off to next. Michael?" George asked.

"Well, I'm on my home stretch. I'll be taking the county roads that parallel Highway 29 as I head east. I was planning for two weeks on the road. But I decided to hold off on going to the Eau Claire area so I'm running ahead of schedule. If I arrive home by tomorrow night, I will only have been gone for ten days. But I'm OK with that. Elaine, my spouse, called yesterday with some good news. She told me that

Encouraging Angels

Simon, our son and his wife, Ali, are expecting a baby. It's their first and our first grandchild. It makes me anxious to get home, so if I arrive home earlier than I had originally planned, so be it."

The four of them visited a while longer as they finished their ice cream and then George said: "We better get this young man home. He's helping our neighbor finish up with haying – second crop. He's in for a long day."

"It's been a pleasure meeting you – Shirley, George and Tanner," Michael said. "And Tanner, I hope you'll enter the contest again next year. You wrote an excellent speech. And you spoke not only to our heads, but to our hearts. Not everyone can do that – but you did."

"I probably will. I hope we'll be assigned a topic I can get excited about. That's what happened this year," replied Tanner.

"Thank you again for what you did for our son," said Shirley. "You've been like an angel, appearing 'out of the blue.' You did for him exactly what Tanner addressed in his speech. You 'put heart' into him – that is, you encouraged him -- and for that we are very grateful."

They bid each other farewell and Michael began his walk to the parking lot.

After arriving at his pickup, Michael drove back to the Sky View Inn. Along the way, he thought: Yes, I should be able to make it home by tomorrow night. Nobody says I must make the trip in fourteen days. And if I get home early enough, maybe Elaine and I can go over to Kohl's and look for baby clothes. A smile crossed Michael's face and he thought about Elaine, home and the prospect of becoming a grandfather.

After he arrived at the Sky View, Michael called to check in with Elaine. She was pleased to report the progress her reading students were making: "Remember the boy I told you about the other night – the one I introduced to a couple of Packers books. Well, he's finished reading both of them and he's checked out two more."

Michael jotted a number of notes regarding the day's activities and then went to bed. As he turned off the light, he sighed and then announced to his darkened room: "It's been a good day!"

www.ingramcontent.com/pod-product-compliance
Lightning Source LLC
Chambersburg PA
CBHW071508070526
44578CB00001B/478